RECEIPT

ALSO BY KAREN LEONA ANDERSON

Punish honey

RECEIPT

poems

KAREN LEONA ANDERSON

MILKWEED EDITIONS

Published 2016 by Milkweed Editions
Printed in the United States of America
Cover design by Mary Austin Speaker
Cover photo by Mary Austin Speaker
Author photo by Jerry Gabriel

16 17 18 19 20 5 4 3 2 1

First Edition

Milkweed Editions, an independent nonprofit publisher, gratefully acknowledges sustaining
support from the Jerome Foundation; the Lindquist & Vennum Foundation; the McKnight
Foundation; the National Endowment for the Arts; the Target Foundation; and other generous
contributions from foundations, corporations, and individuals. Also, this activity is made
possible by the voters of Minnesota through a Minnesota State Arts Board Operating Support
grant, thanks to a legislative appropriation from the arts and cultural heritage fund, and a grant
from the Wells Fargo Foundation Minnesota. For a full listing of Milkweed Editions supporters,
please visit www.milkweed.org.

Library of Congress Cataloging-in-Publication Data

Names: Anderson, Karen, 1973- author.
Title: Receipt : poems / Karen Leona Anderson.
Description: Minneapolis, Minnesota : Milkweed Editions, 2016.
Identifiers: LCCN 2015046648 | ISBN 9781571314727 (paperback)
Classification: LCC PS3601.N54425 A6 2016 | DDC 811/.6--dc23
LC record available at http://lccn.loc.gov/2015046648

Milkweed Editions is committed to ecological stewardship. We strive to align our book
production practices with this principle, and to reduce the impact of our operations in the
environment. We are a member of the Green Press Initiative, a nonprofit coalition of publishers,
manufacturers, and authors working to protect the world's endangered forests and conserve
natural resources. *Receipt* was printed on acid-free 100% postconsumer-waste paper by Edwards
Brothers Malloy.

For Eva, Henry, and Clara

and

for my mother and father

RECIPE

RECEIPT

.....

R E

.....

RECEIPT

....
RECIPE
....

GINGERBREAD
After American Cookery *(1796)*

Three pounds flour breathes Amelia,
America's orphan, pearl-complexioned,

a girly sweetheart but in need of a living:
grated nutmeg, two ounces ginger,

one pound sugar. Spice: she offers
us white powder: something

bitter: *three small spoons*
pearl ash dissolved in cream:

a new chemical leavening
from the burnt-down

trees of Albany. So nice,
so not yeast. So—

one pound butter,
four eggs—laborless: not

eighteen egg whites
beaten to a foam: not fat

to rub into nine pounds of flour,
no sticky miscarriage, no

mother, no child. No need.
Just *knead the dough stiff*

and shape it to your fancy: lady,
orphan, knows how to find

a man: a contract: a fee: the rag

paper cheap; the page gone quick
—*bake 15 minutes*—

with ink—

LAST-MINUTE DATE RAPTURES
After Betty Crocker's Picture Cookbook *(1956)*

My female Virgil, glassy but straight faced, reports:
bees on coke signal they've found more flowers

than they really have: the last-minute date
she set up is evangelical at the end, a shame.

He is sober, I guess, but not enough
to make a go of it, even with the Glorified Rice we ordered

and the plate of tea cakes: *This favorite of men
came to us from a man*, he quotes: nut riches

and filled with sparkling jelly. He wishes
we could get back to that. I, buzzed,

dumb, submit a gate of equal labor, unpearly,
with revolving chores: none of your Wagon Wheels,

Raisin Jumbles, Hermits on the best blue plate.
An empirical kitchen, stainless and useful.

The tools for ascension—the whisk, the rasp—
get his distaste, the mystery out: I'm a literalist.

We split the check. Others here seem
less damned over strawberry fools.

I might rather be them, either one:

one transported, one merely good with a spoon.

Hi Lo Cookie hook,

butterscotch chips, margarine

blond nylon matinee wig

Miracle

cash-money's

another skimpy assistant,

pouring smoke,

a couple of doves,

hand sex, a little homegrown

the words and

imitation;

the real one;

you will feel it:

Everyone has some
trashclass taste, some

and what's his? Is it

instead of butter, the

for the fridge, a taste for

not mayonnaise,
the whip of

dusty con: yes,

yes, the rabbit, the hat,
and some sinisterman

cheap as cheap. The dove,

and later the sophisticate bit
with the canned-soup
camp, some sleight-of-

to smoke, kohl-lined
lashes left in the sink. Say

see what happens. Not
vanilla or its witchy
hang on for the kink,

you'll get better
than some sweet feint.
Wait a minute, and

amazed: ashamed.

PIE

If not by date, by book, by recipe,
then by pie, tattooed, cherry-lush
in the shattering crust I know by hand,

by heart—the garnet gone silk through slits,
the rolled-down skin over salt, rolled down
again, the press of the thumb as it rips

and drapes, undress arrested,
now lifted by heat to the light,
on which you could read,

now vellum, now welling with red,
the kiss of the needle, which if
you missed in your hurry, I guess

now cool, you'll see through slicks
and sheers of juice the sign I pieced
from crust through red, through cover,

through sugar, your name,
you stitched to it.

HOLLYWOOD DUNK
After Betty Crocker's Picture Cookbook *(1956)*

Whipped cream plus onion: a spread for almost-
married Americans, deviled hams dressed up,

mid-chickflick. I guess it might incline us
to service, seeing Grace's Famous

Makeover in Parchment, Handsome Man's
Helplessness on Toast Points. The careless cool

around the staged pool party, engagement
of the rich and pink, endlessly instructive

as my wedding bowls roll by. Part of me
slips behind the white velvet rope,

imagining myself an extra on set:
jut-breasted fifties dress, period piece.

If not a star or guest. If just the dip's
vegetable, chewed ragged by the end,

almost horrorfilm: I need to fit
in that satin dress? I need to say what? If I

had coated myself in cream, my in-laws say,
I'd like me better. "For Anyone Who's Ever Been . . ."

intones a voiceover: a man, white, middle class
and up. OK, fine, I'll watch it all again.

Maybe it will be more fun
with my apron on.

RHUBARB

Unreciped, unlooked up
and sudden, in our yard, pieplant
as supper, the leather-leaved stalk
with sugar dipped up to taste
from the old starred jar as if
no parent were there, as if
we had no plans, having never
planted the plant but found
it out back and odd at the cut,
thready-tipped with dirt,
but it's done at the point, hot source,
the sauce, which should have been red
but is not on toast, the thick
dry stalk surrendered
to heat, and the sweet
made pulp, and we, deep
pink.

BETTY CROCKER COOKING SCHOOL OF THE AIR

Beaten by the recipe, I hear the stars: disarmed chatting.
They love the same foods as me, wondrous colors: lime

chiffon, ruby-red dressing, stuffed-with-perfection
salad. The hours spent out at the kidney-shaped pool,

I assume, improve the taste of their pies, but none
will say so, I hope, to me on the radio, hot at home.

So slow, the directions on how to stay newly wed:
marshmallow, movie, coconut, marriage, whip cream,

baby, mayonnaise, baby: the basics,
my whitewashed ranch slopped down in the canyon.

Flattened and nasty between takes, the brown cake falls
and the water table swamps my foundation.

I hope they are sad, pandowdied and dumped.

All the great tips (the bread-crumb coat, what little kids eat)
but what I like best is myself calling in: like them:

a voice: costing time.

THE COMPLETE COOKBOOK FOR MEN
(1961)

Listen, call on the Method, Fred: you are steak,
Beetpink on the inside, beetcold.
Outside, you are grilled to black.
The world is not made of what you thought.
Consult your feelings on this. Are you
Listening? How much longer do you wish to cook.

ASPARAGUS

Minnows of the air, swallows
and later bats, untatting the garden's
lace of gnats and mosquitoes, and at
the garden's edge the fungi, smoke
and ink, fringe-gilled, raw-capped, ragged
and still in veil, the havishammed,
unlike ourselves, not bud, not born,
not bridal but spores, a net drifting
down to rest on everything, spade
and fork and glove, before the flower
bursts its stem, the rush of green *how I
love how I hate this place we've made*

ASPARAGUS TIPS
After Mastering the Art of French Cooking *(1961)*

We snapped sudden + double
+ phallic + local, a couple

that ended in pieces, the story
asparagus raised was never

resolved so cruel + sad
as the mother who wanted

rapunzel + paid with the child
she always wanted bitter +

fiddleheaded, buttered
+ mathy before its scales

had grown into feathers + *is this*
what you wanted said coldly

over the boiling water,
a reptile ending just

as we broke into birds ≠

These recipes tell us *Mix well*. Or *Bake*
till done. Some dumb sun blighted this land,
no, you did; no, you. The receipt

for repairing damage: shape batter
into bells. I can't. Add salt to taste
to the dough. OK, won't. Make

a well in the sand and knead
till elastic. And how to do that.
Incorporate the fat in layers;

careful not to overdo it;
you're overdoing it; exactly; I am;
kneading hand over hand

over hand; now, *Fight well*,
you two, as the kids watch the world
burn down. *Did you fight to save it?*

If not, start over. A moderate-

hot oven, like hell. *Like hell*
you do. Like love songs, someone
to blame: it's all you, you, you, you.

When they all mean me: God-mad
at the water drying up
each day in us, in the well.

CROWN OF GLORY FROSTING
After Betty Crocker's Picture Cookbook *(1956)*

Inside, all the icing is undone: the butter
cream's split, crumb coat, glories, accessories—

allegretti, tinting, little animals, candles—
scattered around the dirt-brown cake, the sugar lace

as if the gods gave us frost, then left, scraped

less to a sexy fresh divorcée of a species, more
red-hot mess, housecoat open, not caring.

Jesus wept. No more a fat meringue tearing up
next to a bowl of cold white dressing: a relief

to show the holes in this ozone's coat, this now-
no-longer-listening shamble, grey roots showing,

polycotton dress for the heat. Candy in the hand,
not for decorating: a sickly melting blue mess,

but who will know. All those years of hearing
It's not so bad, honey, don't worry. The plastic

polar bear was for a farewell cake: a glacier: your ex:
needing coconut snow: now you can say: go

scatter your glory somewhere else.

COMPANY
After The I Hate to Cook Book *(1960)*

How scattered I am postspouse, with company coming,
in Florida in my earthquake gown, in my eelskin slingbacks

and electric mink stole. I tried to make
puff paste with sweating hands: butter

in the KitchenAid, covered in Everglaze;
apocalyptic looking and no one to stall.

Now egret feathers, alligators, and gas
are gone; polar fur coats are all vintage

or bottle jobs and the corn is crawling
even in the Bracken and the Glades.

But I'm up and dressed, at least; I make

with this doctored lambskin a dish of myself:
big hair, lippy, lush, horny. I'm going

to breathe in and replate the takeout
again, shake cocktails. I'm going to spread swampy,

an idea, mangrove of the air.

VENISON
After The Wild Game Cookbook *(1972)*

Are coin of a past realm, old fashioned
and gamy after the calmer meats,
debeaked or ink splashed, dumb;

the deer inflate across his neighborhood,
the new boyfriend, tick-rich, collared, sterilized,
but still a numinous slew of brown boxes

built on stripling legs or the sun strained divine
through their ears' big pink shells—
bark being skinned, teeth in a blind.

The park of hinds and hounds is now highway;
their tawny is ordinary to the lawn.
It won't work with him or with him.

A congregation. I regress. I diminish. I'm gone

from wolf to bad fawn for them, men:
trash tin at the heart of silver, picked off;

ringed; delicious sapling in the mown—

LADIES' NIGHT
After The Moosewood Cookbook *(1977)*

Dear Ultimate Good Kid, Gold Digger:

The water's coming and it wants to break
    you into life.
It's easy to raise myself up
    from my sad past:
single lady on a night away from the romance book
    I was Vegased and white-riced
and lived the end I read about
    in Sin City Wonder Bread.
Now, later, I'm goddess at last by virtue
    of the bulk bin: the good,
not totally global, but somewhat earthier,
    making white pink itself,
buckwheat, kasha, brown wool tights
    pulled over blueblood
and gilt. And inside? I hope
    it's better than science class.
Girls once of a kind, hostesses, ermine,
    slim-fit, unsad
unmen, but now maybe a man
    can knead the bread.
It's true biology will fool you when
    it can, its pants
unbuttoned, but look. See
    the blood
flood its organs? That means I love someone's
    something and hate
to keep it hid, a way to make men firm
    despite their skirts
and soft hair. Learn from
    your ingredients.
The dough will rise in water
    just to show

it's alive or it's aerated or so
      the animals
inside can try to breathe, expand, mate.
   The story's,
in short, still carnival,
      though we traded
Vegas for cats and hemp. What happens
      to those girls frozen
in the bin of whole wheat,
      doing good and digging gold.
A great hot.

CARAMEL CAKE
After The Silver Palate *(1982)*

It's a great plot, hot sugar.

Simple: the bubbles are loose as change.

The mange of white on the stove's knob

is a declaration of sex to come, crystalline, boutiqued,

sterile metal. Accruing as it turns. One could sit here,

secretarial, watching the nice but boring pot caramel

and never get as much as high-end butter on a finger,

as I now call it, investor.

Or you could trade those colonial fruits abused, swollen

around the pips and scarred,

tarred with something fancier than icing: just make a batch after
    your briefs:

high risk over sabayon.

You need to compound your sweets,

profitable as in "Lukins and Son" or even "Rosso and Daughter," company with all the right products

but never too much ambered by the heat. Oh, no,

I know I said I'd watch this pot all day, but I can't.

Not worth my time. I may hate the stocks

always clambering up and down the chart,

but they look great over the top of a whiteboard cake, untasted;

maybe glue to some shaky foundation, a weekend getaway, turning

leaves, all that. Maybe later.

The hummingbirds eat, unsophisticated, raw sugar water.

Which I can't serve for dinner either. I'm getting older. Get in line

at the great new shop. Pasta, pastry. Lingerie and clocks.

Wherefore caramel is

our human fragment

as nylon thongs are, fire meshing the market

to these rotting globes of fruit.

                              Expensive as hell, the wait—

BEANS AND SQUASH
After Chez Panisse Cooking *(1994)*

Your ingredients as they are
in the wild: the deer are ocelots
in the marsh, fierce and spotted; the bear
are sleepy deer or beaver;
I am the ex-vacation house
trying to be healthy, to remember
what is real; make it up
to the kids who ninja and dog
themselves on Halloween,
posed by our dying maples,
blood-red and sugar; a thin, silver
rain to deliquesce the paper and felt
of their store-bought bodies; within which
I fixed nitrogen and cheating
syrups; which I should purge;
indistinct, I hear the animals in the sand
of the vanishing coastal ground—
I forgot to shore up the genteel grind
of perfection before the big disappear;
not hot dogs on sticks, not brats;
they seem sad; each bean examined
as it goes in the pot; each gourd tight
in its orange skin; so seasonal; and lit;
matinal but melting in the dark and
goldly from the inside; kids likewise.

TV DINNER
After the Food Network

Worst, the split left us partial—our bats mega or
micro—his place or mine. Smoky, sac-winged,

and pallid we gothicked the art
of a dinner for kids and one grown-up.

At one time. However ghost-faced,

faintly moustached, there was comfort
in the old separate spheres; the turkey in its divot,

the cranberry, neither from-scratch pie nor Twinkies
for dinner, whereat the fruit and meat

got ate together, beside the TV, microwave,
Child breaking up into static as the doors

bang the new cable back and forth; now Ray or Lee;
can we go outside? *No*, I said; then

I don't know, trying to make it up. Once,
it seemed better to be a leaf, partial, subordinate,

a unit in the duplex than the old whole, don't
you agree, or maybe you don't. Or maybe

I'm not talking to you anymore, static and spectral,
maybe not.

PIZZA NIGHT

Kale, local, wilting in on itself.
Organic egg: a frittata except
you have only a corruption of
conventional cheese. Something
that was asparagus; some oil
you built with pesticidal
spices. Olives full of black
holes. If you had made the right choices,
you'd hardly need to mix matter
with what doesn't matter. Yogurt, plain,
but from a big box. You wouldn't
use a faulty cog in your rocket,
so why this scattering of rotten
parts? Strawberries, unseasonable
and furred with silvery fungus,
a really bad mistake. Corn
cut from the same metallic cloth.
The cheese magnet-blue with mold,
gravitational. Or would you, did you,
unschooled and awake, imagine
all the chemicals revolving inside
you, blame antimatter for how
much quicker it sucks in? There are
the mushrooms gleaming white
in the dark, collapsing and slick in the bright
air. All at once you are: needing to feel
full of the worst thing you can
without meaning anything: dark, a star.

CORN
After The Omnivore's Dilemma *(2006)*

1. Corn (*Zea mays*)

means grain, worn-out countrified
joke. A core that won't quit,

a miracle sheathed with leaves

and big evil, a rental home in the husk.
The expert says I am now heirloom,

which sounds, well, ethical and unsexy;
good science says I need to keep building,

creeping grain by grain closer to being
a platinum queen. Either way, I'm dried-up

silk in the future, heaving monotone sighs
through the pork's pink sockets

and the beef's. The strain glows strong
along each side of the roadside stand,

the gene trying hard to freak, joke
like your mama, like American teeth.

I porn to look like the source of things,

get back in the kitchen: blond meat.

2. Smut (*Ustilago maydis*)

And the consequence of corn:

smut: up a dead old pole burlesques

a corn snake, towards the hole of the birdhouse,

the old testament the birds never learned.

My mind denies its own badness to feed

itself junk: cows mad *fine*; ergot *sure* in the rye.

But to be smut: to know I am by-product—

bit part in the stalls of a monochrome studio—

is to make myself disgusting hot. I remember

now how the porn plot goes: Silver Queen

meets Old Mold over and over.

The field of corn knows it's not fine.

The fungus rewinds and goes harder this time.

I need to decide which one I am.

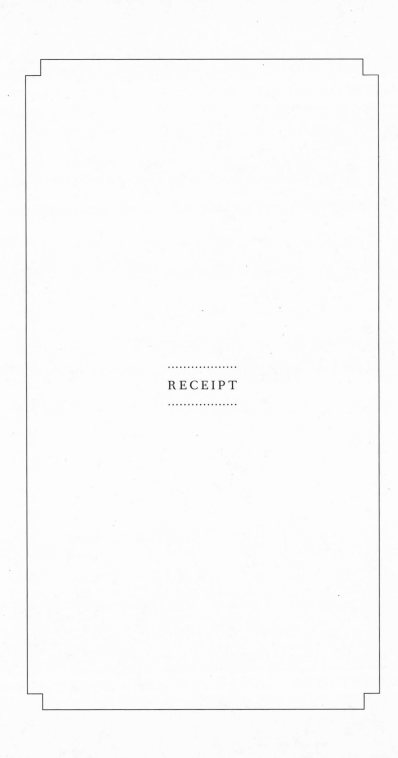

RECEIPT

BEAUTY NAILS ($39.95)

Mom laughs, fingers fungal:
above each manicured hand, the posted
consequence. A violin
or dash of caviar, bedazzled
man, champagned car. To you,
my dear; every finger a sin.
On either side of the salon: Seed
of Life Christian Bookshop, Planned
Parenthood of Maryland: ignore,
desire, ignore those what-you're-fors.
Beauty is a cast-iron bull with painted-on
hooves at the antique mall. Still,
to a woman or a man say *here I am,*
your child, and they're pinned—wood
to your iron will, slug to your
romantic picnic. Each diamante
has a hole within the lacquer: each
design's glam: god's nails to your unplanned.

FINAL SALE ($245.94 Lord & Taylor)

I could have had the heavy fall of a dress
cut correctly, the sweater designed to mask
the ass. Loot blessed by the mannequin's
upturned hands. *Who steals my purse
steals trash*. The men's department end-times
more rapidly, but who cares. Women's coats
with their murderous trims and swings,
everlasting feather collars: on sale for a reason.
Can I steel myself to graft the insane
to the classic: shoulder pads, the cocktail
cut, the holy A-line. Wings sprung into being
and fading with the season. Outside, I finally find
the trashbirds feeding themselves in the dumpster,
sparrows and grackles, timeless sable and green.
Spent tags, plastic hangers cracked like ice.
Scattered fries, lice and oil. They drain that chance
till I can't say what steals my birds. My purse. My trash.

PAID ($3,678.53 Capital One)

The dachshund and the deer are one.
—WALLACE STEVENS

In this world, too late. The dachshund
yelps and springs in on impala's legs, squeals rubber wheels
and steel to catch the flying debtors,

                      so here I am. A therefore, a thus,
thrushes pumping melody in the dark, no clockwork lark
at all, the interest. I may choke on it; I may wish
never to have been an artist with cards, a platinum voice
in a plastic 'verse.
                  But see, I'm now definite debt,
an existence built on dinners out and clothes, men,
and the management of myself. That's my kind
of work, if you must know, with your *Pay here!* and my *You wish.*

Therefore, bill me—you will—for time off, the day paid
and satisfied with the paper cells of the wasps' silver
nest. How the single girl survives. How the sterling shivers

in its box to hear the voice's bell. May I speak to your manager,
Trish? Hold my account and the check wings
through the mail to toll myself. Don't tell my mother. How about:
instead, on my death, I bequeath you my capital, my plans,
my dachshund aspirations:

to fly as well as I wish.

FALL ($14.99 CVS)

To catch someone; old-fashioned; use your private jet;
your head; hair bump't up in front; collar unreg'ed,
the strawberry of confusion; wonderbra;
false calves; flier miles; lashes; contacts
in violet; hanging sleeves; codpiece;
express line; culottes; falsies; business sense;
business class; love of kids; the demi-
mondaine; and the vamp; the platinum club;
coquette with her hat and her tragedy;
her shortcuts; her shot; at the bigs;
the bangs; with her shoes and her heels
and her lashes like wings; in lines; in planes;
and platforms; when what I need; on paper; is work;
my contract; my gamine; my hat;
my halo hat; to stop pouring hot air
into the air; as if insane; as if by chance;
I'm shot with regret; for deception;
for consumption; the conception;
if by not having wings; and requiring flight;
my head; should also go off.

STARLINGS

The most beautiful clothes: iridescent black
over Snarl Call. I wore the soft Sparrow

to the store, borrowed the Crow to bag food;
the Chickadee to the masquerade, the Vulture to the show,

wore my silhouette more raw-necked
and veined. Stare: it's hard

to think of me as the citizen of a star;
I'm no jet-sharp Swallow, no Bluebird's rare,

rosy décolletage, no white breasts
sterling the light, no Swan. I wear the soft gray hat

of the Junco pulled down. But I can,

in Starling, gloss more than one thing:
employee of my own oiled-silk finish,

purple-green trasher of your silence,
reflector and sharp-beaked shredder of

your most gorgeous and boring murmuration:
mine mine mine mine.

SKIRT ($29.69 T.J. Maxx)

God, I said I'd never hobble,
but maybe broomstick or bell—
good to the legs—bubble
or trumpet according to the mags.
A stitch in my time, but tulipy, sunbursty—
or knife and cartridge, alternatively,
with a military skirt, the myth
of the frail girl body underneath,
inside; the old cocktail fork
of good enough/not good
enough, whether at the office
or breastfeeding. I can't
pin up a whole half
of the species. I can't stop.
I guess a good skirt
would help; I guess I'm bleeding;
I guess from the force with which
I pleat myself back to myself.

GRACKLE

of least concern. The corn
(relax, Ma) is not under threat.
Bronze-bodied and bald, though,
means I am; I do; succumb to his
common name and yellow eye and thumb.
Great work, Jack, the others yell
to him. (I'm not kidding
about the thumb.) *Great tail
you've caught with
your purple.* (I'm the tail.)
I forgot that *Jack* means small;
I forgot that *Daw* is a corvid;
meaning that man is a call
and not a promise, meaning that
despite his great numbers
and noisy selves, he may not call.
(I know you said he would not call.)
He is intimate with ants. He is
his own Corvette. And after
the first date, he may call. But Ma,
I'm warning you: I may
because of his great numbers
ignore his calls.

GULL

And fool no one.
To mistake stones
for your own eggs,
which you warm
for ages, then
find out they're not yours.
To think on all
deception as a gift,
coming before
you're dead; another false
pleasure, yet
another lesson. To silver,
to slender, to slaty-
back; to most ridiculously
cleave to site and mate;
to find divorce
selected against; to find
your food in every
place: mussel, bread,
minnow, clam,
fry, the unhinged, prophylactic
jaw. To learn
to catch the fish with the bread.
To learn the hell
of becoming better at it,
dropping your prey
from the air, mangling things
for the sake of your fledglings
and then for fun: to use
the rock against the shell.

LITTLE BLACK DRESS ($49.99 Nordstrom)
After Laurie Colwin

I take you as me, chicken salady, adaptable.
I mean, you're a meat but bird,
celery, mayonnaise? Hardly counts, now

that you're removed from your gaudy
feather trim and sequin eyes. Basic,
unflappable, the dead body—lean or not—

fine at a gala or barbeque. OK, I admit.
Hemlines change and you're the fourth one
I've bought, synthetic, uncompostable,

and department store brand. I'm not
my mother; I couldn't have sewed you up
had I the time. But let's say we all feel this way—

costumed—we have in common
the slimming thing, uniform, funereal.
Undigested by time or fashion.

Consumed wherever we go
without gusto and without
disgust, also.

LACY ($292.06 modcloth.com)

Oh, I'll get your bone lace, tatted on a fish's spine
for the bride, for your carnival. Inside, though,

I sew you to your shadow, crude
and machine made, torque your honeymoon,

bad fairy at the wedding. I come unstraight,
counting ones for thongs and straps,

unsunned and stripperish. I look
forward to your indoor tan, your SUV,
and your fertility kit. I can't knit

(too patient
for me that click and twist) and   unbridesmaidenly
I never loved the pillow—talk nor cool

percale—but oh,   if let outside, I can macramé some ozoney
throw for the bed.   Can you seat me near

the door please, at the big, ahem, event?

Mom's fault. I have this thing   for holes.

DAVID'S BRIDAL ($0.00)

Not fair, say the pollinators: marriage equals horse and ass,
not corn that has to self. The deer avoid the protest;

they want the wedding to last, with the orchard
unattended, whole and half bowls of flowers left

to attract the bees and the smooth peachtree bark
lit red with impractical lanterns. Other charms

than the natural must answer this equation:
the dollar and the coin? Uh, broken into each other.

The insurance man and his pen? Multiple and cheap
as policy, flung one after one. Even bees,

say the protesters, proxy-sex the flowers,
their legs quick as fertility clinics. The deer,

whisper the guests, mount mechanically
whatever's in season, man or woman.

The baby's hardly inevitable. In the church,

beforehand, a long line forms before the women's
room before they all use the men's.

MERINGUE ($3.25 Pâtisserie Belge)

Less   than   egg   sugar
I'm built around   a café   house   held up
by rent   car's   choke   leased
the snow on   credit ·   iced
weddingdress   hospital   white-flowered
lawns   clovered   gowns
crinoline everything   trembling
on the cusp   of breaking   debt
fracking   me   that I stay
elastic   under the crust
the limit, deflating   crystalline
or liquid   when they want   or need   Alaska
Mom   lessor   stretched   I ask you
how   much more   can I   be

CLEARBLUE EASY ($49.99 CVS)

Last name: Smith. First born:
Adam. Says this: *Luxury weakens to destruction*

the powers of generation. In women,
I guess, good at decadence. I don't care

about the undying plastic of the monitor.
Over the counter, eyeing

the young mothers and their easy
multiples, I saw through each brake:

time, money, men, bad eggs
of the aged and done. The arguments

go to waste, shrink-wrapped
and warped to the stick. Stimulated,

I might keep up. If fertile, I probably
shouldn't be: birthrate, currently low

as the national, blue as a mantle,
pooling out from all those golden moments

of global ascent: the burgher Madonna,
I got my angel in the stone window,

a nurse on the phone with insurance,

with my cup and gown, my blue plus.
I disappear from the sentence.

Is it covered, she says as she looks up.

PIGEON

No gull, I loved the dead ones, too,
skins to feather my nest.
When these ones come, I won't
be anymore a coward, a cheater,
a leaver, informer, haunter, fancier,
salt, shot, coat, toed, mailed, drop:
I'll be all throat: all mother: fiery
blue-green: I'll *make oppression bitter*:
I'll feed them all there is: the milk
of my face, my crop, my stony
birdy body gilled with worry, pleasure
of statistics; I'll watch my helpless
fellows getting feathers as if
they're all I've got.

EPIDURAL ($25.00 copay)

About to lose feeling, pain is a fiction
of the spine, friction that hasn't

happened with the four apparent outcomes
according to the baby manual: demon chick; stunned

grub; angel; textbook. ALL HAIL THE UTERINE
says one shirt, packed just in time, in 1973;

HELP ME DAMMIT the other. So clear
to meet the needle and its chefish friend;

the fine, knowable hand and its bright,
silvery currency at this mostly effective

dinner party: come in and scrub yourself.
I am about to serve your economy

an addition, which I, apparently,
shall trash, shall love. The needle the instrument of.

MADONNA DEL PASSERO

I demonstrate the sparrow:
icon of us, mirrored, fallow,
a sea of dull brown and female,
the thin leash around our necks
snapped by a fat baby:
                            your fate, if you,
like the rest of us, remain dependent,
pregnant with it: the evidence that god
will kill even the worthless, the unformed.

                    But, look, we could be more,
alight in our own places, set fire
to our houses with a stolen cigarette
winged glowing through the rafters; could mate
for life but get, you know, around.
Could flood the City, and then, just as sudden,
leave it bereft, its barns and malls all skeletal—

                    Could be not spar nor spare but spore,
us, small and alone on the roof. Not just sing
in the broken chorus but to
each other, *chirrup*, a necklace of ourselves,
everywhere, each strung, yes, but each body, skiff;
each wing, oar.

GOSPEL ($0.00 Bed Bath & Beyond)

Instore is sweetly general, TV and soft socks;
back at home, a damned shame and me
always fucking it up. *Is Love in Your Home?*
Is Your Eye Always on the Sparrow?
Should I squat in my nest, god help us,
while the minutes break up into shit?
Repel the better neighbors? *Have date night*
sometime at home. Sure there were
no flowers at my board, no cultivation
in my floor or my mopped toilet.
Dishes stuck with crap even after I washed
and dried them. *Make home a baby haven!*
I'm gone. Help me, going foreign out
to bed and bath looking for the boxstore
beyond the fucking box. *Keep him*
wanting more. I want nothingspecial—
no echolocation, no clean corners,
no big chest to please my man.
Make it new for a happy
home! Just this one thing more
I haven't found yet goddammit to get.

That is exactly what I got.

JAY (~$0.00)

For sale: feathers on the ground;
if your children (~3)
find and collect them; they
are unsentimental; of value;
of use; always blue; the blue
being structural; a function
of light and angle; and of flying;
and not your wishes, not your love;
but pragmatic, the crest of feathers on
the head; the precise portion of
aggression (~4) needed
to thrive minus the energy
(~20) to wave them; if out
of misguided economy
(~100K), you decide
against the purchase of a private
plane; unmagneting the ad
from the sale; and opt for Jay
(loud; loves bottlecaps, foil;
the flash and jabber); then that will be
the result of the mismanagement
of yourself; ad exceeding function;
(Silvery-Throated, Purplish-Backed);
approximation; and they will be everywhere,
plush-crested, azure-naped.

DOM ECON ($120.00 College of
Home Economics)

Look to grandmother for order:
herself a graduate of Troy
Orphan Asylum, she finds
the practice baby, Bobby,
excellent training before
he is fostered out: econ
of the domestic kind
to school oneself in later,
with her own man and boy,
her own day's plan (an hour
for loving, canning Mondays,
dustpan handy). When
your work is done, it's gone,
said the House Mother, and that
appeared on the exam; save
your sentiment for some
other establishment.
Before she graduated
she refused to learn one
simple lesson: Your Household
Is Our Nation, So Record
Your Faults to Remedy
Them. This was the point
of the orphan, forgetting:
Bobby bit, but she wouldn't
save the tooth he sent.

CROWS

I hate all my accounts:

boss and employee,

seller, consumer, whatever.

You are what you're called—

is that fair? Outside, things

seem better: the specific flip

and slit of that poisoned toad

and you're not dead like it,

just more pearly, pink.

There is the virus, yes,

of everywhere. There is

the big stick nest; the spring;

bobcats, owls; an insistence

of fungus. We are quitting

being us like the chick

learning flight's math:

a dress of iridescence

falling slow from the tree's hook,

a brain unfolding with

the air's resistance, calling

this, this.

.....
RE
.....

FAIR

Two kinds of fair: carny and perambulator
of the local: shiny peppers on paper plates

and buttercream-silk goats: Lizabet & Hope
among the floral displays gone south:

please enter again, this was very strong,
next year. A staged race of pigs in felt vests

picked out in red, green, blue around a track,
shivering a ring of fat kids used to this .

easy choice: commercial, delicious fries
or the sad white bread of the VFW barbeque.

Right among the sloe-eyed dirty cow hose-down,
a tired show horse to pet. Sort of oversold

at the 5 buck K9 demonstration; 4H got a thousand
for a rough old hog in red second-place satin.

Dad explains: *Claire's photos won because*
Claire's photos were best. It's that fair, the big grey

hair of a tufted chicken, the mascaraed rabbit that
no one gets to touch to mold you from the fantastic

to the rational: *I would like to thank God for this medal.*
Down at the midway end past the chainsaw bears,

the Old People Tap Dance Show, and the bee man
in the ag tent, madly pointing at the holes

in his rigged-up hive, Mom inspects busted latches
and the blanks between boards and wires,

the scuffed blue of the Tilt-A-Whirl's shelf; on which
is the kind of fair you could get used to;

all places being equal to the blast of bad rock
and the rust-metal floor, a flat Coke no one would want,

ordinary; just one boy's or one girl's sweaty hands
on offer, unspecial.

FAIR

Shut up to hear the copper flip
of their hearts through the air.

In my flash, the warm
wings of bats are dollars on

the market's strings. I followed the, well,
best practice: silver gelatin

to augment my retirement
with photographs; the bats cheat

the swifts, fill the house we built

for swallows. It's another small
economy our kids discuss, um,

ungenerously. I tried to demonstrate
interest, saving, doing anything

at all. But it was always an endless

birthday what-do-you-want: *I want*—what?—

it not to rain when it's, of course, raining.
And now the same old *I hope I don't*

lose it—pause—*all.* Our foil

I shake out and roll in the drawer. The photobooks
of Chartres, Notre Dame, inept, underlit,

are there. It's patience, I say, that saved us.
From what. I'm waiting with my camera here

and no bats. The kids can't help us—the phone cuts

into dinner, like the circus or church,
blaring, sequins—they have to work. Then

they don't call at all. Then the yard's
a silvered blank as the moon comes up.

I've saved nothing. I want to shoot,
but can't, the warm vault of dark,

their wings I hope up there.

FREE MINUTES

Frogs calling all-network:
across the marsh's mall:

bored, out of air con, but money
on the phone: green-

silver skins turned in
for high drone or The Twang:

battery undead, yet,
by egret-beak mom

and her snaky neck,
wrecked by no ring,

no repetition unto
death: bath & body

works: arrested sex
and the signal: a single:

fake vanilla-scented candle:
cell: divide or mend:

hell no: texts
the female: boneless:

colony of before-
foreplay at the mall's

door: the boys' noise
saying nothing but

their gestures making:
the world's hard bill.

ECHOLOCATION

Winter culls: the rose gold of beeches
glows like script, gilt, a fixed

alloy river running through
stripped trees, candles lit

in paper bags; a cheap trick; a bad writ;
immiscible: the old and the new:

the owls' and the bats' maps traced
through the ancient trunks, mice

in the scents laced through the leaves

and the insects' sad endless mesh.
No contracts, prepaid. We all want

to be sieved and saved, a signal,
an emergency. Wishing the self

would stir while the others hold still. While

the others give way? While the young
make the mash, make calls, their *available*,

their *fail*. As we fall at the foot of the stairs
and wait. As the alcohol lifts and rings

through the air. In the winter, still.

FIRST JOB

Summer girl, you are radium
to this failing fabric shop, you drill the faille
when the farmer's satin tanks,
sell off the angel and the sharkskin

as if the customers always
wanted that. Sales-tween, twin,
no hopsack hollow-cut velveteen
will bury us, you said; half manager,

half woman curved in the furry fearnought
and Janus cloth. So what if they buy
only charmeuse and twill—khakis
and bridesmaids, the fools in a bifold magazine.

It leaves us the bombazine and crash,
butcher linen and brocatelle; I bought
to sell, yes, but I can double the world
out of doors with what we have here:

lawn and grosgrain, bark-crepe, birdseye.
I'll be the duchesse, you the duck;
hard and soft, the shop finally for sale
as I turn the lock and notice you're gone:

your dress and autocracy: apostrophe and
democracy: marble and the mousseline.

RETIRED

and stiff, we stalk the dead mall: Leaks
Galore, Bare Ruined Racks, Etcetera.

And Claire's, of the cheap gold hoops of sun
and mouse-skull bracelets, frost cracked.

Still intact, the fungus lushly slotting
the Gaps, a Lotto of cervine molars, bats

soundproofing Rafters on shifts above
the Big Lost Lots. For us, the stainless

sale section is sparrowed, better now
for sex; for us, all weather is fine:

all is food court, all big echoey bathroom.
The sapling guts the floor's plastic

tiles at Borders, the wind unplants
the plastic trees. The fountain writhes

with larvae, renovating the rain.

CURRENCY
After Adam Smith

Two of me at market: I see Zea,
tinny jewelry and micro-mini, or May,

in cap and dress to her shins; sustained
grain by grain, though, a monoculture;

the rows ever closer and the girls
from which they came more or less

rubbing up against themselves. Clonal,

the teenage economies: smoking pot
and spinning wool, small change snaked

from the register, rain's silver green
in the streams and then crisp yellow, maize to sugar

and white teeth to veneers; in the horse
and buggy, in the spinners of the car

that won't stop and the poisoned river
of bills and coins. Century to century,

corn's a better measure; year to year,
it's silver.

SO, NATURE

is not at all that hetero. Monoculture of oaks
drop their seeds hard on my porch.
Here the sparrows mentioned by my friend offend
uniformly the passersby of the urban kind.

My first time down to the luxury of mass trans,
I'll cross the class border and sit there, the picture
of the middle: whitish, shod, odd without truth.
My friends, we are all Ruth in this cabin,

we hurtle amongst the corn, hopelessly single,
unsingular kernels in the foil. I tried to make the country
come to me, but I normed in this flimsy pod,
crib of the future, uniformly uncurious. I wanted a stern mom,

to be one, I wanted to storm home and back to work,
instead of this jerk and click, this injurious
raven on the brick station, who takes no notice
of my passing capsule; the recalcitrant, ashy bees; a stork

stalking the trackside wetlands. I hoped the trip
would unbox me from the diesel into ether,
but I can't just get heeled up and go back to the club.
I will probably pet my domesticates

and avoid thoughts of the war. Uncobbled
from the quadrupeds, now my own horse, condo'd
and mobile enough, I guess, hobbled to my car,
silver in the garage, pretty close to my neighbor's. Friends,

I doubt I can speak of us, actually, without
thinking of the tractor mags he's so hot about,
his plain black mailbox, my being into it.

FIRST HOUSE

Unforeclosed, rabbits' ears are salmoned by the sun.
New windows, hardwood, subfloor: perked porn.

Bees have restored the holes they left in the porch.
Dead red squirrels restored by corn; morning glories restored

by the shovel that severs and buries, severs.
St. Inigo, let me, please, soldier on,

secure this multitude of ants and boards
before the universe finds and deploys me again.

A dead junco is a grey feather boa, strung on the bush.
Its head is a hawked black hole in my imagined mortgage

and warred-for mornings. No matter. I won't want to go out.
Poison glory to spout from the twisted blue trumpets of home.

RETIREMENT HOME
After George Herbert's "Love (III)"

Love Bade Me Welcome in this dumb game

for us, the already-gone. I click, with difficulty,
on white death, blue-black, and the little brown

bat. My avatar blinks and waits at the lip
of the cave to enter and sit

and spread my disease. It seems
like school. It seems from the bills

I am already enrolled here at this home
with its one computer

and its murmuring food. The nurse
has turned her back: *Do you*

want to go in? the pop-up repeatedly
asks, meaning the fungus is now

on my hands and then on the inhabitants.
Where is the button for *Already in*

and *Wait as they drop from it,*

sick with my clicking and their breathing slowed.
Nothing to do but sit with my neighbors

as the beeping goes on. The problem, as I've
said, is not in the room or computer

but the echo: I did sit already.
I did eat. No question. I know now how

to close this window. Breathing, heartbeat,

plot in the chart. In the beep that I am.
Do you want to go. No. Do you want.

Again, no.

DECORATE

I know how from TV: declutter the ocean like a plastics drawer.
Stuff the poles back up with some snow;

you can use the cheap stuff. Then donate. The shelves should go
and shade the sun that makes a dry scar

of the stream and riverbed. They just hold junk. You'll need a new pump
to keep it going, a cord and a cover for the cord

to make the floor seamless now with the walls, so tack up
a fax of the woods you've used; bamboo and a random

pattern of cork tiles to draw the eye. Paint the brick and staple burlap
across the walls for a global feel. Add

sustainable mosquito netting to the bed and use the savings to go
for the Deluge Showerhead. Find the oil that is practically

fracturing your floor and sell it for some glued-down, beautiful tile,
almost solar with heat. Cheap, if it holds. Disaster, if not. It's simple:

if the bones of your house offgas, then coat the bones.
Next: new bones.

ESTATE
After George Herbert's "The Collar"

No more: I was always a materialist, child-free,
less the cash I spent on glass crushed

with dust and oil prints. Each red coat big
with my image; each untouched emergency phone;

each set of dishes rimmed with gold
and licked by my collective pets. I fed

the deer off them when I wasn't dead. I bred
the bats in a house I built. I augmented

this property by stuffing the barns
with sleds older than myself; struck

with dim baby carriages and ice-
fishing awls. Subject

to nothing; no idea but myself
and my animals.

It was just what I loved
in the flat-faced portrait

and sandy old rope.
Fitted or not:

big heavy keys to nowhere. Little
blue candles. A groaning board. Someone

auctioned and bid and then I was back
in the world. Abroad

in the garbage bags
thrown in the back of her car,

in the bolts of my fabric, my perishable food.
Orpheused by the dog, the bags torn

to shreds. Me. A careless child driving.
My buyer. *Good stuff.*

She said. *You*
can get, she said, *me later*,

into her phone, her held-out
palm. I got her. Lord.

Thus was I spread, was I free.

VERTUE

After George Herbert

Tremble, everyone.
We all must die.

No matter how nice the day.
Further and further from

my body, I have grown large
with fashion, receded, fallen,

inverted the leg of mutton,
the melon, the envelope sleeve,

thinned into my youthful parts,
a box of scattered sweets,

me; and also I die, a bat,
wings slimmed to paper

by *Geomyces destructans*—torpor

of the corporate—which may not
spare this part or self. But were

I not myself—my kids,
receipts—did I let myself

go—my sleeves, eats,

cells—might not
I give. Might not

it all unknit—a little—the kids
—less—me—less—

us— now—live—

Acknowledgments

Barrow Street: "Crown of Glory Frosting" (published as "Receipt: Crown of Glory Cupcakes"), "Betty Crocker Cooking School of the Air" (published as "Receipt: Radio Cooking School")

Best American Poetry 2012: "Fair" (published as "Receipt: Midway Entertainment Presents")

Books That Cook: *The Making of a Literary Meal* (New York University Press, 2014): "Gingerbread"

Colorado Review: "Madonna del Passero," "Starlings," "Grackle"

Counterpath Online: "*Can-Opener Cookbook* (1951)" (published as "Add to Mixture"), "Paid"

Delaware Poetry Review: "Asparagus," "Rhubarb," "Pizza Night"

Denver Quarterly: "David's Bridal" (published as "Receipt: At David's Bridal"), "Beauty Nails" (published as "Receipt: Beauty Nails")

Fence: "Ladies' Night" (published as "Proof")

Interim: "Free Minutes" (published as "Cell Bill"), "Venison," "First House" (published as "Receipt: Real Estate")

New American Writing: "Last-Minute Date Raptures" (published as "Recipe: Last Minute Date Raptures"), "Hollywood Dunk" (published as "Recipe: Hollywood Dunk")

Phoebe: "So, Nature" (published as "Receipt: The Future is the Metro"), "Corn"

Poem-a-Day, Academy of American Poets: "Company"

Seneca Review: "Fair" (published as "Receipt: Midway Entertainment Presents")

terrain.org: "Retired," "Fair," "Decorate," "Vertue"

Western Humanities Review: "Caramel Cake" (published as "Recipe: Caramel")

ZYZZYVA: "Retirement Home," "Estate"

Thank you to Dina Bishara, Suzanne Buffam, Janine Caira, Jennifer Cognard-Black, Bruce Cohen, Jeff Coleman, Matthew Cooperman, Stuart Davis, Alex Dimitrov, Gina Franco, Alice Fulton, Roger Gilbert, Laura Gray-Street, Kate Greenstreet, Leslie Johnson, Michele Johnson, Amber Kuzmick, Jill Magi, Fred Muratori, Chris Nealon, Mel Nichols, Karl Parker, Srikanth Reddy, Paul Sawyer, Jonathan Skinner, Brandi and Roger Stanton, Stephanie Strickland, my colleagues and students at St. Mary's College of Maryland, Maureen Thorson, Lyrae Van Clief-Stefanon, and Maggie Vandermeer, as well as the editors who chose my work for publication. Thank you to Daniel Slager, Patrick Thomas, Connor Lane, Mary Austin Speaker, Joey McGarvey, and Casey O'Neil at Milkweed and to Hadara Bar-Nadav for her insightful editorial comments. Special thanks go to Sally Keith, Dan Beachy-Quick, and Mark Doty. I could not have written these poems without the everyday faith of Jerry Gabriel, Mona Anderson, Greg Anderson, and Amy Swanson.

KAREN LEONA ANDERSON is the author of *Punish honey*
(Carolina Wren Press, 2009). Her poems have appeared in
ZYZZYVA, *Fence*, *Colorado Review*, *The Best American Poetry 2012*,
The Ecopoetry Anthology, and other journals and anthologies. She is
an associate professor of English at St. Mary's College of Maryland.

INTERIOR DESIGN & TYPESETTING BY
MARY AUSTIN SPEAKER

TYPESET IN FOURNIER